# THE COMPLETE FLUTE PLAYER
## BOOK I
### BY JOHN SANDS

MIDPOINT
PRESS

Designed by Howard Brown
Photography by Michael Michaels
Arranged by John Sands

**ACKNOWLEDGEMENTS**
My wife Jean for her patience and encouragement. Louise Holmes for the
modelling and Harold Clarke on whose teaching the book is based.

Flute supplied by Pearl Flute Company

# CONTENTS

# INTRODUCTION

The beauty of the flute lies in its ability to sing like the human voice, so what better way to learn than through the practice of songs and beautiful melodies.

This course uses a step by step approach, adding new notes as they appear in the tunes, but always with the basic idea that the flute should sing.

In Book 1 of The Complete Flute Player the student will learn to produce the sound and apply it to popular melodies, and at the same time, learn the rudiments of music as they occur in the pieces.

By the end of Book 1 you will have learnt to play:

**All My Loving...**
**Where Have All The Flowers Gone...**
**Annie's Song...**
**And I Love Her...**
**Michelle...**

And many more tunes which you will enjoy.

In the past most flute methods have been confined to using folk tunes and excerpts from the classical repertoire, but here we have a tutor based on sound teaching principles, using tunes you know and will enjoy playing.

The tunes have been carefully chosen for their scale content, and the rhythms have been adapted where necessary to suit the student's development.

The Scale and Chord page at the end of the book can be used as a daily exercise page as the student progresses through the seven keys used in Book 1.

## THE RUDIMENTS OF MUSIC

Reading music is easy if you learn with a 'step by step' approach. This page will tell you all you need to know to complete Book 1. Use it for reference as you progress through the lessons.

Music is written on five lines, called a **stave**.

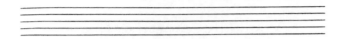

The stave is divided by vertical lines into **bars** or **measures**.

Double bar lines indicate the end of a tune or section of a tune. Double bar lines with 'dots' mean the last section is to be repeated.

Occasionally, when the repeat is from the start of a piece the double bar line and dots are not shown at the beginning of the music.

The length (or duration) of notes is shown in this way…

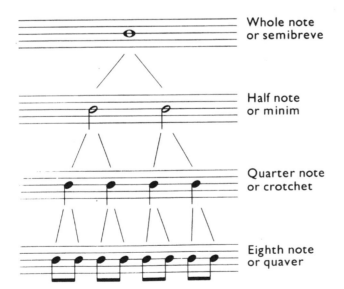

Whole note or semibreve

Half note or minim

Quarter note or crotchet

Eighth note or quaver

A dot after a note increases its length by half as much again. Therefore:

Dotted minim lasts for three counts

Dotted crotchet lasts for one and a half counts

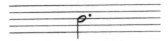

The first seven letters of the alphabet are used to name the notes.

A    B    C    D    E    F    G

Continuing upwards from the note 'G' we arrive at another 'A'. The distance between the two 'A's is called an **octave**. (This applies to all notes). For example:

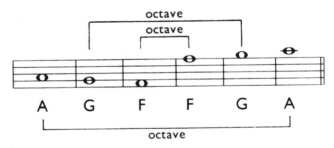

octave

octave

A    G    F    F    G    A

octave

The note 'A' above the stave is on its own line. This is called a **ledger line.**

Ledger lines can be added above or below the stave.

The tunes used in this book have either two, three or four beats in the bar, this is called the **Time Signature** shown at the beginning of the stave like this…

$$\frac{2}{4} \quad \frac{3}{4} \quad \frac{4}{4}$$

The signs used to denote 'rests' (or silences) are:

| Four beats | Two beats | One beat | Half beat |

The sign at the start of a piece of music is:

**The treble (or G) Clef**

This tells you that the second line of the stave is 'G', therefore all other notes are relative to this.

A scale is a succession of notes in a set order of tones and semitones (or half tones).

One tone is made up of two half tones.

### The scale of C Major

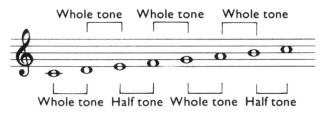

To lower a note by a Semitone we use this sign ♭
This is called a **Flat.**

To raise a note by a Semitone we use this sign ♯
This is called a **Sharp.**

Sharps and flats are put in front of the notes.

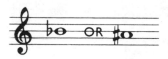

When the sharp or flat is put at the beginning of the stave it is called the **Key Signature.**

And this means that all the notes on that line or in that space will be affected.

Sharps and flats affect notes in all octaves. For example:

All notes on the 'B' and 'E' lines and all 'B's and 'E's written above or below the stave have to be flattened except when this sign is put in front of them ♮

This is a **Natural Sign.** It restores the note to its original pitch.

That is: a flat would be 'raised' by a semitone and a sharp would be 'lowered' by a semitone.

A **major chord** or **arpeggio** is made up of the First, the Third and the Fifth degrees of a Scale.

### Major Chords I III V VIII

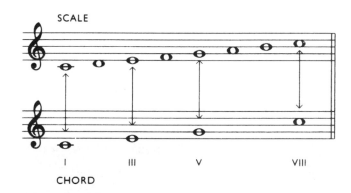

Notes on the same line or in the same space can be **tied** together to prolong the sound.

A **Slur** is a curved line over two or more notes of the same pitch and means that only the first note is tongued.

7

## ASSEMBLING THE FLUTE

The flute is made up of three parts:
**The headjoint, the body, the footjoint**

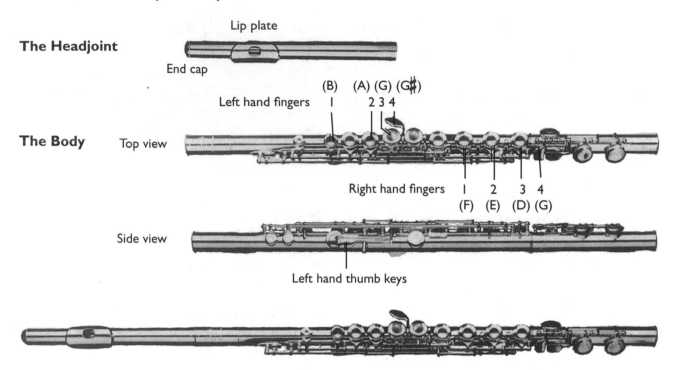

**The Headjoint**

Lip plate

End cap

**The Body**    Top view

(B)   (A) (G) (G♯)

Left hand fingers   1    2 3 4

Right hand fingers   1   2   3   4
(F)   (E)   (D)   (G)

Side view

Left hand thumb keys

Note: the position of the Lip Plate in relation to the keys on the Body and carefully adjust the 'Footjoint on your own flute until it matches the flute in the photograph.

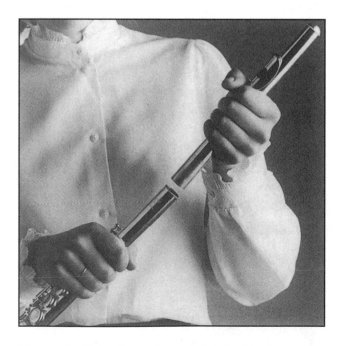

**How to hold the flute when putting the headjoint in position.**

**How to hold the flute when putting the footjoint in position.**

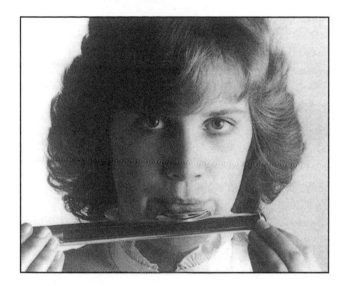

## Producing The Sound

Using only the headjoint blow a thin stream of air across the embouchure hole.

The open end goes to the right of the body.

The lips should be relaxed, and in a slightly turned out position.

When a clear sound can be produced, cover the open end of the headjoint with the palm of the right hand.

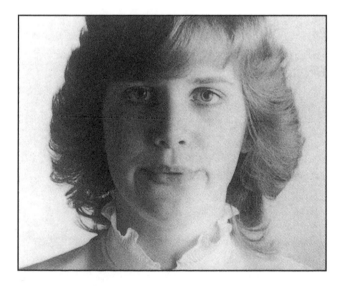

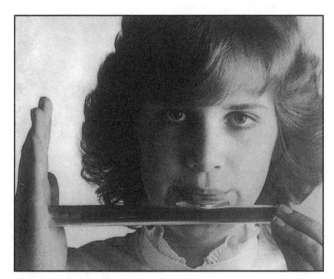

The sound produced will be lower in pitch and hollow in sound.

By gently pushing the lower lip forward you should obtain a higher sound. But **do not** blow harder.

This action of the lips is the most important part of flute playing.

It is advisable to look in a mirror when practising with the headjoint.

You can then see if the embouchure hole is in the centre of the lips.

The stream of air should be like a thread coming from between the lips.

Cover about a third of the open hole with the bottom lip.

The flute can be played either standing or sitting, but which ever way you choose, it is important that you have the correct posture.

Study the photographs carefully and try to copy the positions shown.

Take note of the right arm, it is lifted away from the side of the body.

This will help your right hand position.

You will notice that the player's left arm is raised slightly.

This left arm position will prevent you from letting your head drop towards the flute.

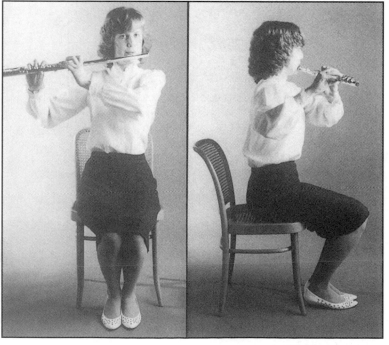

When playing seated, the upper part of the body is erect.

Do not lie against the back of the chair as this will restrict your breathing.

## A Word About Breathing

To play the flute requires a good supply of air.

The best way of controlling this air is from the lower part of your lungs.

And the easiest way to get it there is to push your stomach out as you draw the air in through your mouth.

A little practice without the flute will soon get you breathing correctly.

Assemble the flute as shown in the photograph.

Now practise producing the sound without touching the keys. (Support the flute with both hands as shown).

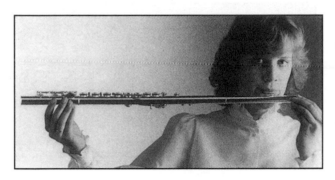

Although in the photographs above the flute is not held in the correct manner, it helps beginners to blow their first notes.

The note produced should be C ♯ (C Sharp).

If you have a keyboard available, check it with the black note next to middle 'C'.

This note is usually rather sharp in pitch but this can be corrected by pulling the headjoint out from the socket slightly.

You will play this note again later in the book, but the flute will be held in a different way.

You are now ready to play the first note using keys. Place the thumb and first finger of the left hand in the first position shown in the photograph. (You can still use the right hand as support).

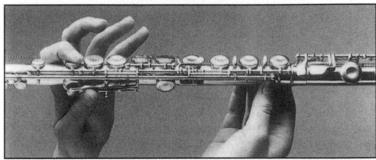

This will produce the note B ♮ (B Natural).

Hold this note using as little air as possible. (Remember our 'Thread Of Air').

To repeat a note on the flute we use the tongue, as in saying 'to'.

Try to keep a steady stream of air, as if you were playing one long note.

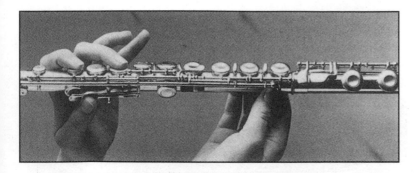

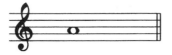

When the note B can be produced clearly, and without using too much breath, place the second finger of the left hand on the A key.

This will give you the note A ♮ (A Natural).

## Practice for B and A

Semibreve or whole note

Minim or half note

Crotchet or quarter note

Repeat each two bar section keeping a steady rhythm.

Try tapping your foot on this exercise, remembering to keep an even tap.

This is called the beat, or pulse, and it will help you to feel where the notes are changing.

Choose a speed of about one tap per second and keep that speed throughout.

Each tap will be one crotchet.

When both B and A can be played with a clear tone, (remember to keep the lips relaxed) place the third finger of the left hand on the G key.

This will give you the note G ♮ (G Natural).

## Practice for B, A and G

When you can play this exercise with a clear sound and steady beat try increasing the speed, but still keeping it even throughout.

The next note we will play is C ♮ (C Natural).

This is produced as for the note B, but with the thumb removed.

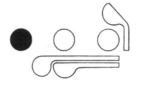

**Practice for C, B, A, G**

| | | | | | | | | | | | | | | | |
|---|---|---|---|---|---|---|---|---|---|---|---|---|---|---|---|
| I | 2 | 3 | 4 | I | 2 | 3 | 4 | I | 2 | 3 | 4 | I | 2 | 3 | 4 |

In this short exercise we introduce a one beat rest 𝄽 and a dotted two beat note 𝅗𝅥. which now gets three beats.

Keep a steady stream of air and try to breathe only at the rests.

You are now ready to play your first tune. This is **Barcarolle** by Offenbach and is in **¾** rhythm. That means there are three beats in each bar.

Dotted minims   𝅗𝅥.   Three beats

Minims   𝅗𝅥   Two beats

Crotchets   𝅘𝅥   One beat

## BARCAROLLE (FROM "THE TALES OF HOFFMANN")

BY: JACQUES OFFENBACH

Practise singing the tune (you don't have to know the words just, 'LA').

Keep a steady rhythm and breathe only where you see ✓.

You will notice that you will breathe naturally at the points marked with ✓. Now try to carry that same feeling of singing when you play the tune on your flute.

Our next lesson uses the first finger of the right hand.

Make sure that the first finger and thumb are almost in line with each other, and keep a nice 'curve' on the finger, so that the pad of the first finger falls on the centre of the key.

This, combined with the left hand fingering for 'G', will give you the note 'F♮' (F Natural).

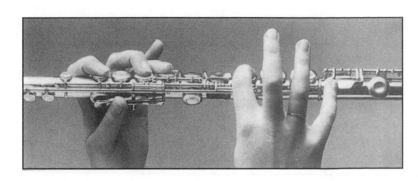

This note is best approached from G.

You will notice in the photograph that the little finger of the right hand is also in use. It must rest on, and open, the first key on the footjoint.

This is called the 'E♭' key, but at the moment it is used as an extra support for the flute, and does not affect the note we have just learned.

Here are two exercises using the notes and rhythms we have learned.

Make sure that the first note is clear and 'vibrant' before you proceed, then play each exercise many times until the fingers fall naturally on the keys.

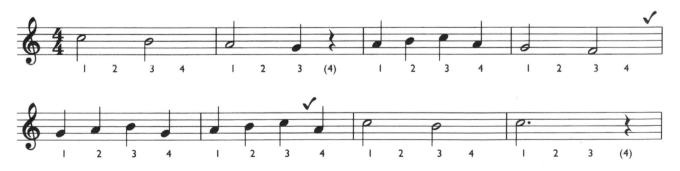

Tongue each note in these exercises but do not stop the stream of air.

This exercise is for the 'lips'. Keep the lip in a turned out position, and try to play the five notes in 'one breath'.

The curved line over the notes is called a **slur** and means that the first note only is tongued.

Play it first with a rather quick crotchet beat, and then gradually slow the speed to make it a study in breath control.

When you can produce the note 'F♮' with the same clear sound as the notes which you have already learnt, you can move to the next one which is 'E♮' (E Natural).

This is done by adding the second finger of the right hand as shown in the photograph.

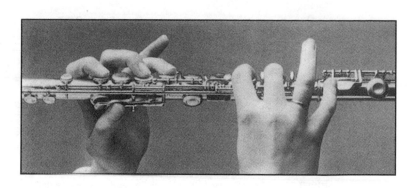

Again it is best to approach this note from the notes already learned.

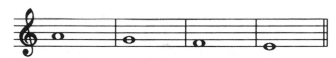

Hold each note as long as possible, but **do not** 'Blow' hard.

Remember our 'Thread Of Air'.

The next exercise uses all the notes we have learned so far.

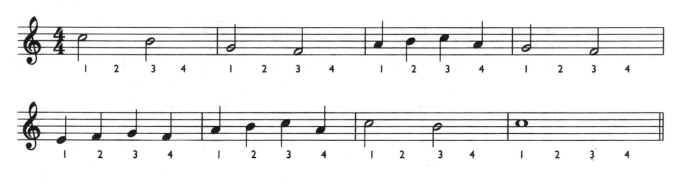

We can now introduce **Quavers** or **Eighth Notes** into our rhythm counting. Quavers are shown thus...

Two of them are equal to one crotchet.

If you count them in this way, it will help you to keep them even.

Here is a tune you will know which uses all our notes and includes quavers.

## PUFF (THE MAGIC DRAGON)
WORDS & MUSIC: PETER YARROW AND LEONARD LIPTON

Keep a steady rhythm in this exercise. Think of a 'clock ticking'. Each tick will equal one crotchet or quarter note. And of course two quavers or eighth notes equal one crotchet.

We are now going to use the key for 'F' and add it to our 'B' fingering to produce a 'B♭' (B Flat).

This is one half tone (or semitone) below 'B♮' and is the note we use in the key of F Major.

Repeat this section at least four times. And make sure that the 'F' finger is raised when you play the 'A' in Bar 2.

The next exercise uses both 'B♮' and 'B♭'.

In Bar 5 the last quaver in the bar is also a 'B♭'.

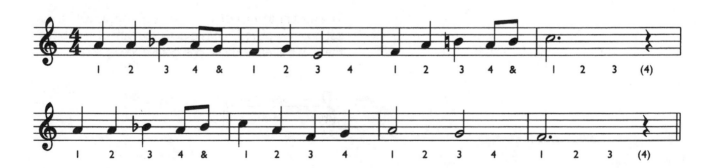

The next note is 'D♮' on the fourth line of the stave.

It is an easy note to produce but make sure that you have the correct fingering.

As you can see in the photograph, the first finger of the left hand and the little finger of the right hand are both away from the keys.

This leads us on to the next note which is 'E', one tone above 'D' and fingered exactly the same as the 'E' you already know.

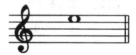

(The distance between these two notes is an **Octave** which means eight notes higher.)

Practise both 'D' and 'E' with the same 'lip position' that we had when we practised with the Headjoint with the hand covering the open end, and producing the higher sound.

The next note we learn is 'F Natural' and, as with the last note we played, it has exactly the same fingering as the 'F' we already know 'one octave' lower.

We can practise these notes as 'Octaves'.

Remember to use the 'changing lip' technique and **do not** tongue the high notes.

Our next task is to change from 'D' to 'E'. This is a difficult finger movement, so practise very slowly to start with, making sure that the first finger of the left hand is down on the key when you play the 'E'.

Repeat this exercise until the fingers move smoothly from 'D' to 'E', then reverse the notes.

Observe the 'slur'. Tongue only the first note in each bar.

We now have a range of notes from 'E' in the Low Register to 'F' in the Second Register.

All we have to do now is to connect them and we shall have enough notes to play a famous Beatles tune, **All My Loving.**

As with the last exercise play this very slowly until the fingers change confidently from one register to another.

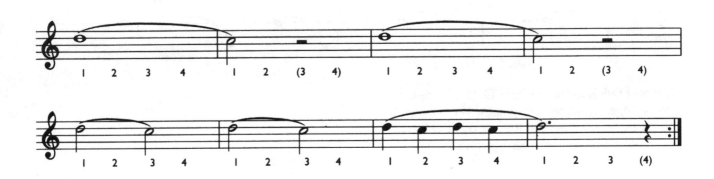

In the tune 'All My Loving' you will notice that there is 'B♭' sign at the beginning of each stave. This tells you that you are in the key of 'F Major' and means that all the 'B's are to be played as 'B♭'s.

You will also see a first and a second time bar.

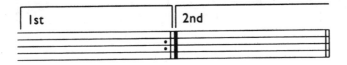

This is a device to save writing the whole tune out again. It means that you play the 1st Time bar, and then go back to the double bar at the start of the tune, and then play the 2nd Time bar on the repeat.

The two notes before the Double Bar are called **Up Beats** and are replaced on the repeat by the same two notes in the 1st Time bar.

# ALL MY LOVING

WORDS & MUSIC: JOHN LENNON AND PAUL McCARTNEY

We can now move on to the next three notes. 'G', 'A' and 'B', As before, they are fingered in the same way as the 'G', 'A' and 'B' in the lower register.

Keep the lower lip pushed forward and **'do not blow hard'.**

They should be no more difficult to produce than the notes just below them.

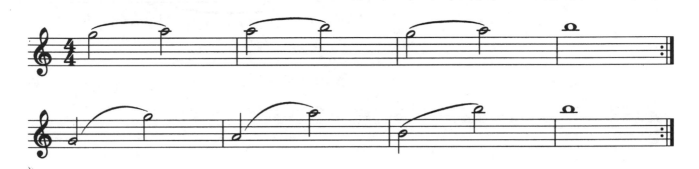

'F♯' (F Sharp) is our next note. This is one half tone higher than 'F' and is played with the third finger of the right hand.

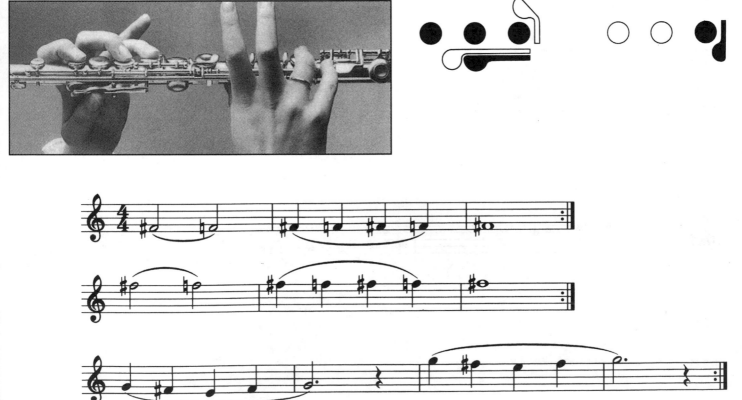

# THE COMPLETE FLUTE PLAYER
# PULL OUT FINGERING CHART

# FINGERING CHART FOR NOTES USED IN BOOK 1

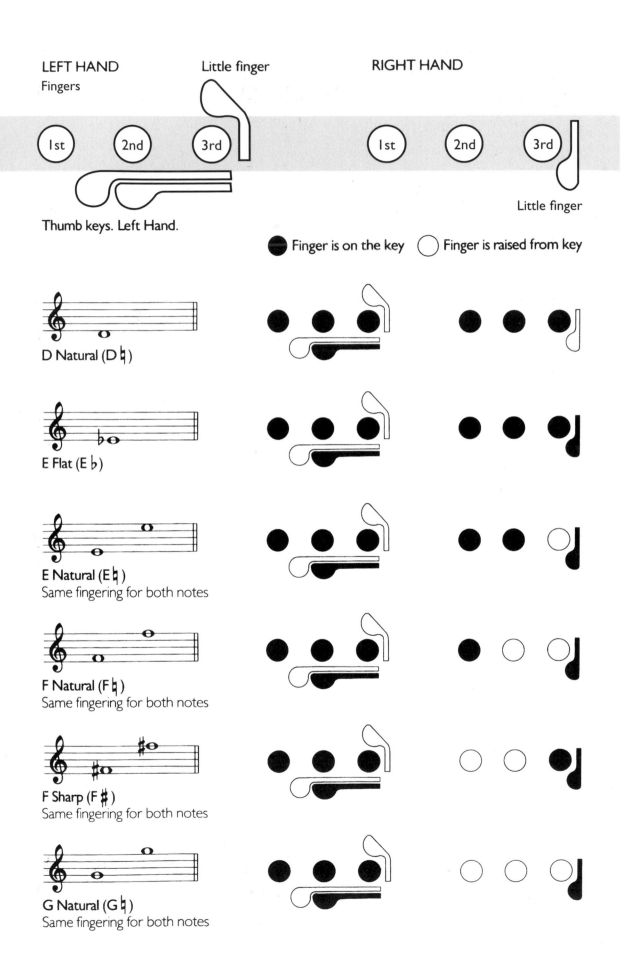

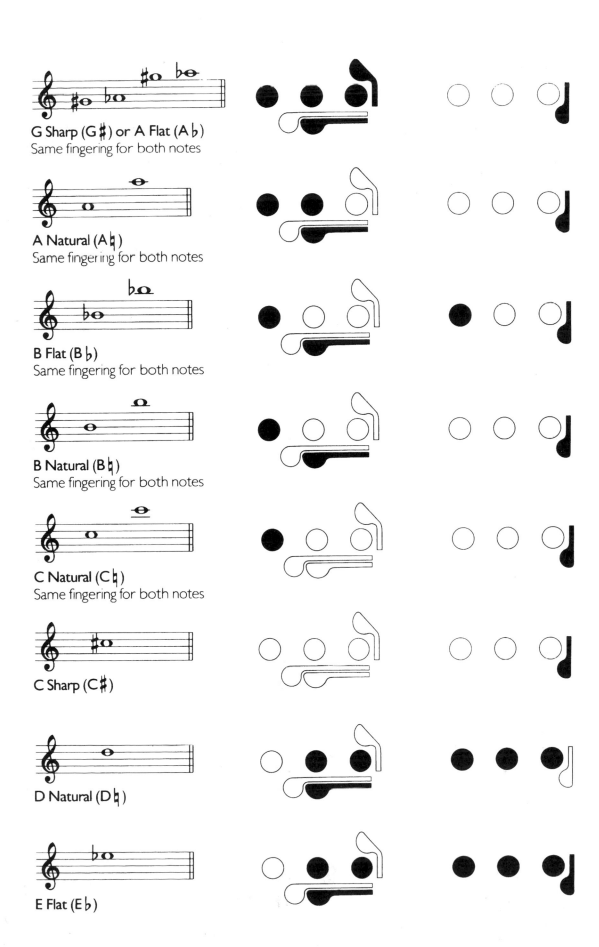

**G Sharp (G♯) or A Flat (A♭)**
Same fingering for both notes

**A Natural (A♮)**
Same fingering for both notes

**B Flat (B♭)**
Same fingering for both notes

**B Natural (B♮)**
Same fingering for both notes

**C Natural (C♮)**
Same fingering for both notes

**C Sharp (C♯)**

**D Natural (D♮)**

**E Flat (E♭)**

With 'F♯' we can now play in the key of G Major.

The sharp sign goes on the top line of the stave but it applies to all 'F's in whatever register.

Play this tune in a singing style and try to breathe only at the breath marks or rests.

Take care with the last notes. The line connecting them is called a **Tie** which means that the second note is not tongued but becomes a continuation of the first one.

## WHERE HAVE ALL THE FLOWERS GONE
WORDS & MUSIC: PETE SEEGER

To connect the notes 'C' to 'D' we remove the first finger of the left hand to give us the note 'C♯'.

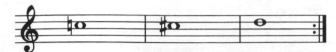

The flute should balance quite easily if you have the right hand thumb in the correct position and the right hand little finger on the footjoint key, as shown in the photograph.

With 'C♯' we can now play a tune in the key of D Major.

D Major has two sharps in its key signature, C and F.

And they are always in this order...

This famous tune is in $\frac{3}{4}$ time. Keep a steady rhythm and make sure you count the correct number of beats in the **Tied Notes**, some of which are tied through three bars.

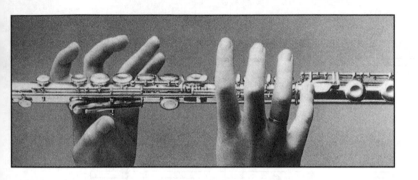

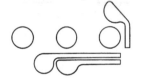 

### ANNIE'S SONG
WORDS & MUSIC: JOHN DENVER

We can now add the note that lies between G ♮ and A ♮.

This is G ♯ (G Sharp), played by opening the key as shown with the little finger of the left hand.

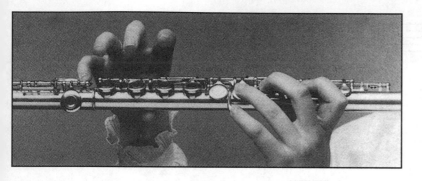

The G ♯ has the same fingering in both octaves.

Make sure that the G Sharp key is closed when you move to another note.

Practise both these exercises many times, gradually increasing the speed.

Take note of the crotchets at the end of Bar 1 and Bar 2. They are also G ♯ s, as an accidental affects all

the notes in the bar on that line or space.
(Sharps and flats which are not in the key signature are referred to as accidentals.)

In the next tune we will use G ♯ and also introduce a new rhythm.

This is the dotted crotchet followed by a quaver.

It is made up of a crotchet tied to the first quaver on the next beat.

And is counted

Or in **3/4** with the dotted note on the second beat.

And, of course, the tied quaver is not tongued.

Take note of Bar 7. The A ♯ is fingered the same as B ♭

This is called an **Enharmonic Note** and means it has **two** different names but **one** sound.

# CHIM CHIM CHER-EE

WORDS & MUSIC: RICHARD M. SHERMAN AND ROBERT B. SHERMAN

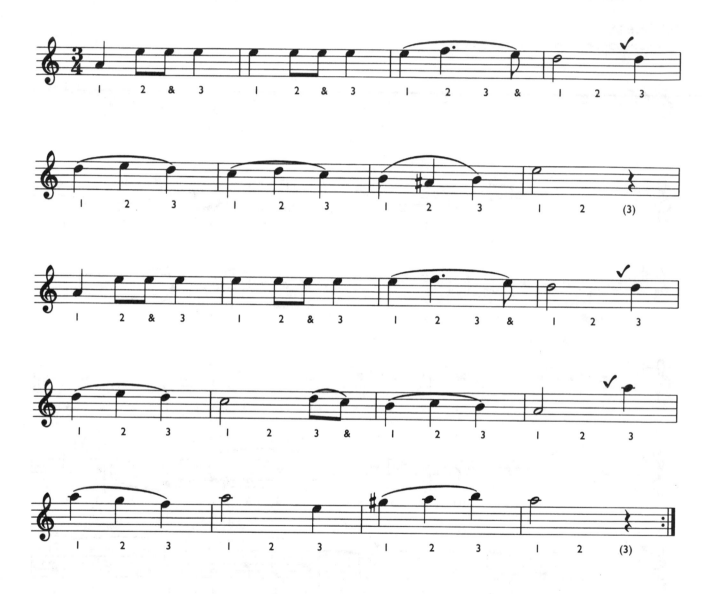

Our next tune will be in the key of A Major, which has the three sharps we have learned in its Key Signature.

They are shown in this order:

Count very carefully when you get to Bars 9, 11 and
12. If you have difficulty, clap the rhythms while keeping
a steady beat with your foot.

## MICHELLE

WORDS & MUSIC: JOHN LENNON AND PUAL McCARTNEY

The next key we will learn is the key of B♭ Major.

This has two flats, B♭ and E♭.

Key of B♭ Major.

Remember that the flat signs apply to **all** 'B's and 'E's.

The B♭ we have already learnt and the one in the higher octave, have the same fingering.

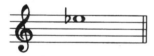

We will learn the E♭ on the fourth space first.

For this we use the E♭ key on the footjoint. Up to now this has been used to help balance the flute, but now we use it in conjunction with the fingering for D♮.

Remember that the first finger of the left hand is raised.

We have a new sign to observe in the next tune.

**D.C. al Coda (Da Capo to Coda Sign).**

This means you go back to the beginning and take (go to) the Coda when you come to this sign ⊕

# AND I LOVE HER

WORDS & MUSIC: JOHN LENNON AND PAUL McCARTNEY

Here is another tune in the key of Bb, but before you play it, practise the two largest intervals in the tune, (An interval is the distance between two notes). They are F to D and F to Eb.

Use as small a lip movement as possible and make sure your fingering is accurate on the D♮ and E♭.

# ARRIVEDERCI ROMA

MUSIC: RENATO RASCEL, WORDS: GARINEI & GIOVANNINI, ENGLISH LYRIC: CARL SIGMAN

E♭ and D♮ at the bottom of the stave are our next two notes.

They are both fingered the same as the E♭ and D♮ we have already played, one octave higher, except that the first finger of the left hand is down.

Our next tune is in a new key, the key of E♭ Major.

It has three flats in its key signature; B♭, E♭ and A♭.

A♭ is the same as G♯ (enharmonic note).

The most difficult finger movement in this key is from B♭ to A♭ and F to E♭.

Practise the next finger exercises and then apply them to that lovely traditional tune '**Lavender Blue**'.

# LAVENDER BLUE
TRADITIONAL

To complete the range of notes covered by Book 1 of 'The Complete Flute Player', we will add 'C♮' to the higher register.

This note is played with the same fingering as the C♮ one octave lower.

Play this exercise very slowly and as softly as possible.

Keep the lower lip pushed forward.

The key that has no sharps or flats in its scale is the key of C Major.

# EastEnders

COMPOSED BY LESLIE OSBORNE & SIMON MAY

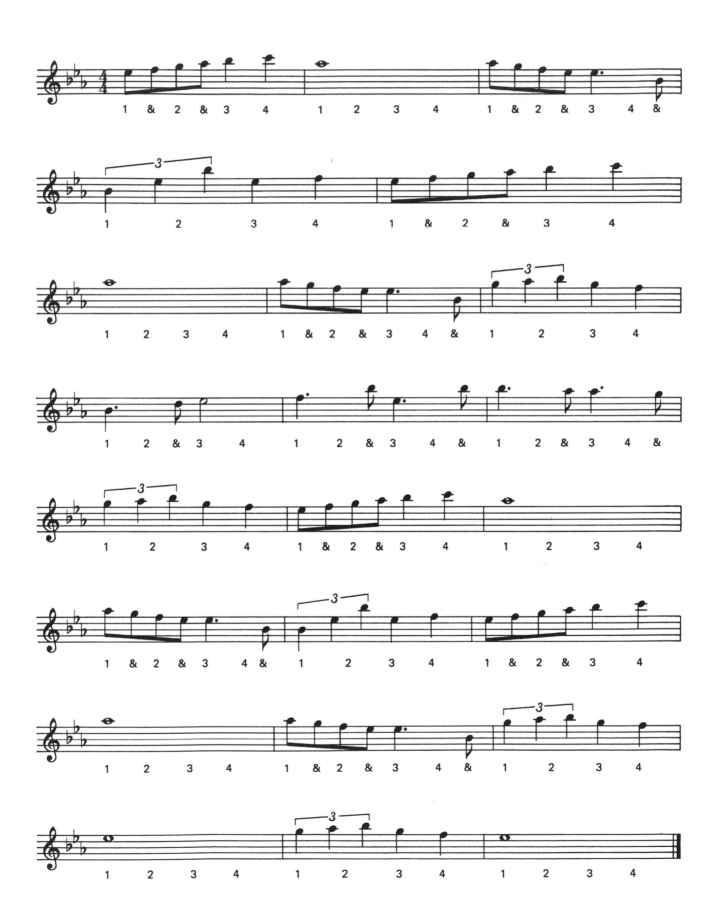

# SING

WORDS & MUSIC: JOE RAPOSO

In **Sing** we are back to the key of G Major.

The 'Rests' play an important part in this tune, so make sure you keep a steady 'Beat' and count through the long rests.

Tongue each note clearly, and **do not** let the sound go into the rest.

# YESTERDAY

WORDS & MUSIC: JOHN LENNON AND PAUL McCARTNEY

**Yesterday** is probably the most often played Beatles tune. It has some lovely flowing runs.

Practise them until they are perfectly even.
Remember to observe the key signature after the bars with the accidentals.

## MOCKIN' BIRD HILL

WORDS & MUSIC: VAUGHN HORTON

In **Mockin' Bird Hill** we can practise the chords from the Scale and Chord page at the end of the book.

The Chords used in this tune are: G Major, C Major and D Major.

Practise them from the Scale page first, and then try to spot them when you play this tune.

## CIELITO LINDO
TRADITIONAL

**Cielito Lindo** is a very popular Spanish tune, in Waltz Time.

Keep the speed lively and emphasise the first beat in the bar.

# SMILE

WORDS: JOHN TURNER AND GEOFFREY PARSONS, MUSIC: CHARLES CHAPLIN

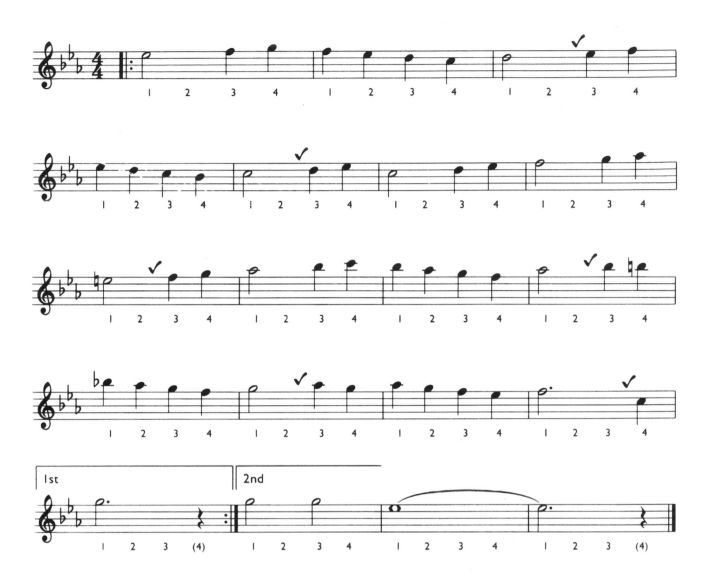

Here is another chance to play in the key of 'E♭' Major with the tune written by the great silent film comedian Charlie Chaplin. **Smile** is a very simple tune made up of parts of the scale of 'E♭'.

It will sound most effective if you play it with a very 'pure' sound. Tongue every note, but keep the airstream constant and the crotchets long.

It would be a good idea to practise the scale from the Scale page at the back of the book before playing the tune.

# CABARET

MUSIC: JOHN KANDER, LYRICS: FRED EBB

Our last piece in Book 1 is the title song from the film **Cabaret**. This is a long tune and needs good lip control to get all the way through without tiring.

Practise it in sections until you have enough endurance to play the complete tune.

The key is 'A Major' so try to keep the three sharps in mind.

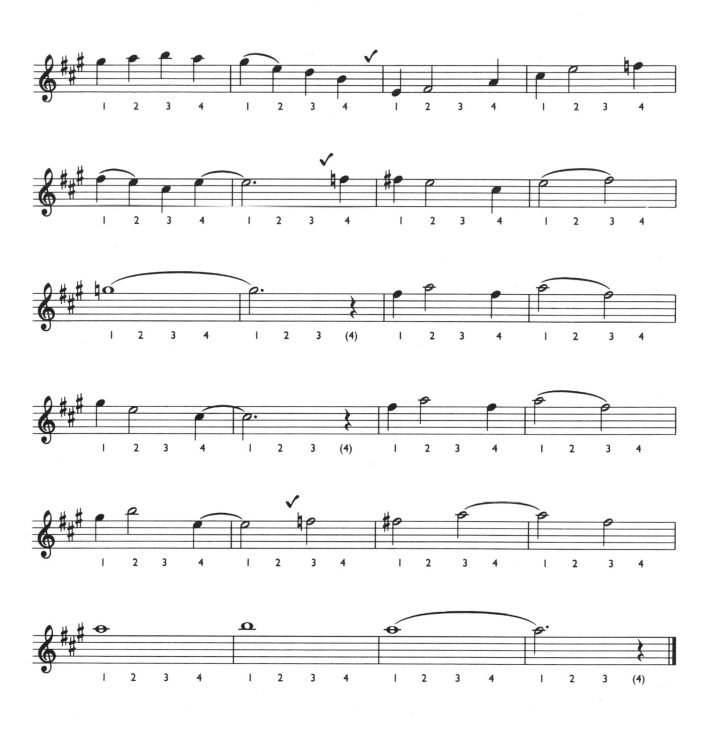

## SCALES AND CHORDS

The scales and chords on this page should be played both with slurs as marked and with each note tongued.

C major

Chord

F major

Chord

G major

Chord

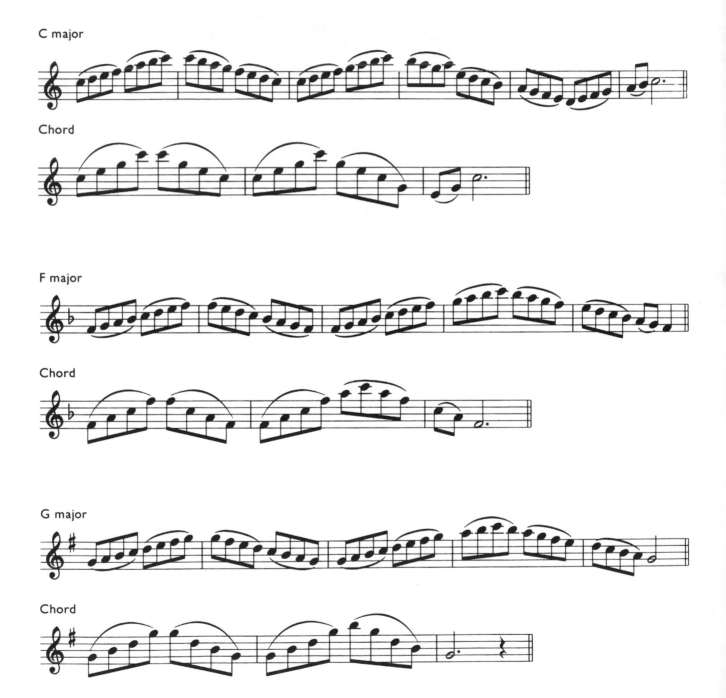

**Bb major**

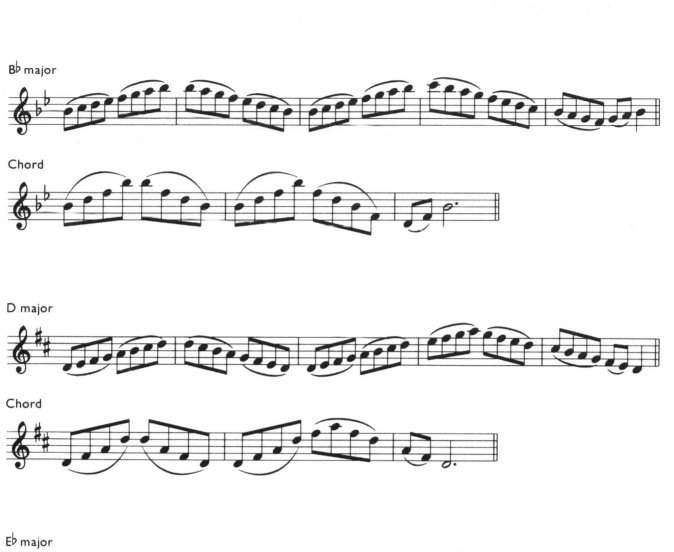

**Chord**

**D major**

**Chord**

**Eb major**

**Chord**

**A major**

**Chord**

## SOME FINAL THOUGHTS

You have now completed Book 1 of 'The Complete Flute Player'.

When you move on to Book 2 you will find lots more interesting tunes to play, but remember that even the simplest of tunes can be played better, so do go back to the tunes in this book from time to time, and try to improve on your previous performance.

Keep striving for that **'pure singing sound'**

But above all, **enjoy playing your flute!**

## In Book 2

You will learn to play some new notes in the high register and lots of tunes to practise the keys and rhythms found in Book 1.

There will be new rhythms including tunes in 6/8 time.

The rudiments of music will continue to be explained as they occur in the studies, and it will include some classical tunes,

The book will contain tunes such as:

**Here, There And Everywhere**
**From Me To You**
**Green Leaves Of Summer**

And many more.

Printed in Great Britain by Printwise (Haverhill) Limited, Suffolk 12/03 (49695)